I think we can all agree that 2020 w
52 weeks long at any rate. Apart fro
any other year.

This is by no means a complete list
come up with that but it is a pretty   .... hap-
pened and what people were talking about.

I have included the list from 2019, to show what a "normal" year
looks like.

Thank you to everyone who took part and listened over the
Christmas period to the A-Z shows on LBC. It is a well worn
phrase, but I could not have done this without you.

The A-Z of 2020

A
Asymptomatic
Antifa
A68A – world's largest iceberg
Amazon's profits
Jacinda Ardern shows how to run a country
ALL CAPS TRUMP TWEETS
Argos stopped printing catalogue
Dr Tedros Adhanom, WHO Director General
Antiseptic wipes/gel
Anosmia, loss of sense of smell, a symtom
"Alas", word often used by Johnson in press briefings
Arcadia collapses into administration
Algorithms decide A-Level results
Anti-vax
Anti–mask
Antidote
Anti-virals
Aeroplanes grounded
Alt-right

AstraZeneca vaccine
Antibodies
Airports left open for visitors – no Covid checks
"Australian-style deal" - meaningless government phrase
Tony Abbott, Australian named UK trade advisor
Army drafted in to help Covid response
Airbridges between countries
Alcohol gel
Jennifer Arcuri, admits affair with Boris Johnson
Aerosol transmission of virus
Antarctica, virus reaches last untouched continent
Ascension Islands, Priti Patel considers off-shoring asylum seekers 6750km away
Arecibo Observatory telescope collapses
Allotments waiting list increases under lockdown
AC/DC release new album
Peter Alliss, golf commentator (d)
Jim Acosta, reporter CNN clashes with Trump
Airbus A380 double deck plane ends production
ASDA sold to Issa brothers, investigated by competition authroities
Anak Krakatoa erupts
Abortion legal in Northern Ireland
Animals thrive while humans under lockdown
Anti-bodies
Alex Allan, standards advisor resigns after Patel bullying report ignored
Hank Azaria of The Simpsons, stopped voicing Apu, re. racial stereotyping.
Acronyms, TYOTA (the year of the acronym)
"Activist lawyers": Priti Patel charge

B
British Airways loses 60% of share value
James Bond film delayed
Kobe Bryant, basketball player (d)

Bat – the source of the disease?
Boeing 747 makes fastest subsonic NY-London trip helped by Storm Ciara
Boeing 737-8 Max grounded
BioNTech
Be kind, social media users urge re. Caroline Flack
Black Lives Matter
Barnard Castle (Cummings' trip)
Billy Barratt, 13, youngest person to win an International Emmy
Bitcoin reaches new high value
Michel Barnier, EU negotiator
"Bung a bob for Big Ben's bong": Johnson's Brexit plea
Bubbles (support)
Martin Bashir Diana interview
Brexit 50p commemorative coin
Build back better, government slogan
Dr Johnny Bananas, one signatory of Great Barrington Declaration
Great Barrington Declaration
Peter Bonetti, footballer (d)
Bill Bailey wing Strictly Come Dancing
Joe Biden, President-elect
Frank Bough, TV presenter (d)
Borrowing, public sector – highest ever
Baking in lockdown
Bournemouth Uni locked down after runner in fitness vest mistaken for terrorist
Ian Botham elevated to House of Lords
Bobby Ball, comedian (d)
Amy Coney Barett, Trump Supreme Court pick
Steve Bannon arrested, bailed
Jeremy Bulloch, actor (d)
Tim Brooke-Taylor, comedian (d)
Bicycle lanes introduced in lockdown
Bush fires, Australia
Bailouts
Kay Burley, suspended from Sky News for breaking Covid rules

Bournemouth beach crowded: "major incident"
Chadwick Bosman, actor (d)
Slaven Bilic removed as West Brom boss
Beirut blast – one of largest non nuclear explosions ever
Honour Blackman, actor (d)
Julian Bream, guitarist (d)
Beaked whale, new species discovered
Banksy artwork removed from London Underground, anti graffiti policy
Burisma, Ukrainian energy firm associated with Hunter Biden
Bounce back loans
Belarus election protests
Bible, Trump tear-gasses people for photo-op holding book
Balcony concerts given from homes during lockdown
BAME more susceptible to virus
Eavan Boland, poet (d)
George Blake, Cold War double agent (d)
Businesses go bust
BBC free OAP TV licence ends for many
Pete Buttigieg, Mayor Pete, US Democrat presidential candidate
Binary, every issue
Borat pranks Rudy Giuliani
Michael Bloomberg spent nearly $1bn on presidential bid, lost
Kate Bingham appointed head of vaccine task force, spends £670,000 on PR
Kate Bingham denies claims of sharing sensitive info with investors
Breakdancing announced as Olympic sport for 2024 Paris games
Beer, poured away when pubs forced to close in lockdown
John Bercow denies bullying allegations
Berlin-Brandenburg Willy Brandt Airport opens
Barbados announces it will become a republic
Bookcases behind everyone appearing on TV from home
Ballet dancer reskill advert pulled
Blursday, under lockdown all days the same
Jeff Bezos', world's richest, wealth "increases by $75bn": Bloom-

berg
Bots, online misinformation

C
Contact tracing
Cyberpunk 2077, glitchy game withdrawn
The Crown, Diana controversy
"China virus": Trump
Tom Cruise distancing rant on set
Dominic Cummings goes to Durham
Dominic Cummings No 10 garden non apology
Dominic Cummings "fired"
Dominic Cummings gets pay rise after leaving office
Crowd noise artificially added to football games
Chumocracy
Cronyism
Jim Corr of The Corrs, anti-masker
Piers Corbyn arrested at anti-lockdown rallies
Melissa Carone, Dominion employee's "drunk" US election testimony
Cancel culture
Edward Colston's statue pulled down, Bristol
Clap for carers
Claustrophobia in lockdown
Cheltenham Festival super-spreader event
CO2 levels highest ever despite Covid lockdowns
Clamp for carers
Cycle lanes
Care homes not protected
Churchill's statue attacked
Conspiracy theories
"Covidiots"
Christmas is cancelled
Coronovirus briefings
Cold War Steve, artist
Chain, Connell Waldren's in Normal people

Crossrail delayed again
Jack Charlton, footballer (d)
Ray Clemence, footballer (d)
Sean Connery, actor (d)
Coughing, persistent: a symptom
Simon Cowell breaks back
Corruption in government
Curfew
Terence Conran, restaurateur, designer, (d)
Heather Chasen, actor (d)
Cruise liners and Covid cases
Cruise liner staff stranded on board
Coronovirus
Corona beer unaffected by unfortunate name association
COBRA meetings Johnson missed
Dr Catherine Calderwood, Scottish top medic resigns after trips during lockdown
Heather Couper, astronomer (d)
Cashless takes over
CHAZ (Capital Hill Autonomous Zone) in Seattle protests
Cher helps relocate Kaavan, world's loneliest elephant
Clandestine Channel Threat Commander, Priti Patel's dinghie spotter
Clinically Extremely Vulnerable people told to shield from virus
Cladding, buildings' fire risk
Child food poverty
Jeremy Corbyn suspended from Labour Party
Chagos Islands, ownership dispute Mauritius v UK and US
Carphone Warehouse close stores
Sarah Cooper lip-syncs Trump on social media
Colonialism and slavery report by National Trust
Cygnus, 2016 report on pandemic preparedness finally published
Claudia Conway, daughter to Trump advisor Kellyanne, social media posts
Canada style agreement, Brexit
Cancer tests cancelled

Ben Cross, actor (d)

Dr Catherine Calderwood, Scotland's top medic breaks lockdown, resigns

Chlorinated chicken

Carping, "this endless carping" about virus test shortages: Rees-Mogg

County lines drug dealing

Coronavirus Job Retention Scheme

Contactless payments limit rises

Circuit breaker lockdowns

Corner shops, the only places that still had toilet paper, milk, flour etc

China, only country to record economic growth in 2020

John le Carré, author (d)

Covid Marshals

Pierre Cardin, clothes designer (d)

Covid alert levels

Contain, delay, research and mitigate: early govt. strategy

Co-morbidities

Andrew Cotter, sports commentator's dogs videos go viral

Cardboard box carried out of No 10 by Cummings

Cornish pasty substantial meal debate

Ciara, storm kills 13

Christo, artist (d)

Croydon council goes bust

Cytokine storms affect Covid patients

Catalytic converters stolen

Centibillionaire club is now Jeff Bezos, Mark Zuckerberg, Bill Gates

D

Distancing

Deal or no Brexit deal

Delivery slots

Delivery driver shortage

Disinfectant – Trump suggests injecting it to combat Covid

Vitamin D to combat virus

Dominion voting machimes in US election

Dover blocked at Christmas

Storm Dennis caused flooding

Daily briefings: Downing Street gloom fest

Kirk Douglas, actor (d)

Dinghies bringing refugees

Roald Dahl family apologise for anti-Semitism

Dead voters – Trump claim

Dumps, massive numbers of fraudulent ballots appear – Trump claim

"Dishy Rishi"

Diversity TV dance routine includes BLM reference

Dog thefts rise as popularity soars during lockdown

Deep fake videos, C4 Alternative Xmas message

Dentists closed during lockdown

Dexamethasone, remdesivir, Regeneron: Trump's Covid treatment

"Diaper Don" trends after photo appears to show Trump wears them

John Di Domenico, best Trump impersonator

Delay phase of virus response

Debenhams collapses

Bob Dylan sells rights to all his songs

Bob Dylan oldest artist to reach No.1 with new material

Diabetes research, mice treated with electromagnetic fields

Debt, national, highest ever

Spencer Davis, musician (d)

Novak Djokovic kicked out of U.S. Open for accidentally hitting line judge with ball

Dilyn, Downing St dog catches Covid

Daytime TV audience surges during lockdown

Johnny Depp v Amber Heard court case

Johnny Depp dropped from Fantastic Beasts and Pirates of the Caribbean films

Dentists closed

Doomscrolling, the act of reading large amount of bad news online

Diamond Princess cruise liner Covid outbreak

Double Diamond, sheep sells for £368,000

E

Eat out to help out

Equivalence – financial relations with EU post Brexit

Epidemic

"Essex girl" removed from Oxford Advanced Learner's Dictionary after campaign

"Elite strike force": Trump legal team

Jenna Ellis, Trump legal "expert"

Billy Eilish wins 4 Grammies

Empty supermarket shelves

Eyesight test, Cummings' excuse to break lockdown

Exercise, reason to be out under lockdown

Elbows bump replaces handshake

Environmental protests

Extinction Rebellion

E-consultation, a way to see a GP during lockdown

John Edrich, cricketer (d)

Exemptions from wearing mask

Engage, Explain, Encourage, Enforce – police Covid guidance

Erasmus – UK withdraws from student exchange programme

Exponential, oft used word re. virus spread

Emergency terror legislation becomes law

Economy shrinks by largest amount on record

Tony Elliot, founder Time Out (d)

Executions, Trump goes on killing spree

Extensions to Brexit deadlines

"Extra points for getting them in order" Trump boasts re. test performance

Excess deaths

Harold Evans, journalist (d)

Epidemiological: we all learned a new word

Chris Evans, actor accidentally releases NSFW pic online
Excel spreadsheet, govt. using old version misses 50,000 trace subjects
Electric scooters
Eurovision Song Contest cancelled

F
FTSE loses £140bn in share value over the year
Furlough
Caroline Flack TV presenter (d)
"Farage garage" (Kent lorry park)
50p piece minted to mark Brexit
Following the science
Food banks
George Floyd's death spurred Black Lives Matter
Fish
Flatten the curve, aim of virus response
General Michael Flynn, pardoned by Trump over Russia links
General Michael Flynn suggests martial law to reverse US election result
Margaret Ferrier SNP MP beaks lockdown
Facemasks worn under the nose
Fly lands on Mike Pence's head during VP debate
David Frost UK Brexit negotiator
Frogmore Cottage refurb cost repaid by Harry and Meghan
Fans absent at football games
Dawn French takes knee in Vicar of Dibley
Derek Fowlds, actor (d)
Firebreak lockdowns
Anthony Fauci US chief epidemiologist
Anthony Fauci facepalms during Trump news conference
Fairytale of New York lyrics changed by Radio 1
Flybe collapses
Fake news
Fake crowd noise on TV football
Four Seasons Landscaping, comic scene of Giuliani news confer-

ence

Fossil fuel cars sales ban set to 2035

Free school meals

Laurence Fox

Rhonda Fleming, actor (d)

Front line workers

Robert Fisk, journalist (d)

5G conspiracy theories

5G: Huawei banned in US and UK infrastructure

Flexible furlough scheme

Neil Ferguson, govt scientist breaks lockdown, resigns

Flour shortage

Face, trying and failing to stop touching it

Fines for breaking Covid rules

Fomites, surfaces likely to carry germs

Nigel Farage bets £10,000 on Trump re-election

"Form a square around the Pritster" No10 re. Patel bullying charge

Fox found with hoard of 100 shoes in Berlin

Fogged up glasses while wearing masks

Rod Phillips, Canadian MP fakes home Xmas tweets while in Caribbean, resigns

Facebook bans political ads before US election

Fogging: cleaning premises with disinfectant mist

G

Greater Manchester Police in "special measures"

Rudy Giuliani

The Great Reset

"Get Brexit done", Johnson's mantra

Ruth Bader Ginsberg, US Supreme Court judge (d)

Nigel Farage spotting dinghies

Philip Green's Arcadia collapses

Bill Gates' microchips in vaccine conspiracy theory

Guardians – name given to Trump's Space Force

Andy Gill, musician, Gang of Four (d)

Glastonbury cancelled
Peter Green, musician, Fleetwood Mac (d)
Gwrych Castle stands in for Australia on IACGMOOH
Romain Grosjean F1 driver survives horror crash
Dave Greenfield, musician, The Stranglers (d)
Graphs, endless, Downing Street briefings
Michael Gove defends Cummins, says he also drove to test eyesight
Great Barrington Declaration, anti-lockdown document
Grouse shooting exempt from rule of six
Government guidelines re. Covid
Google Classroom
Henryk Mikołaj Górecki, composer (d)
Gender Recognition Act reform rejected
Glock 19, pistol Dominic Raab's bodygurad left on plane
Good Morning Britain boycotted by Number 10
Government boycotts challenging TV, radio interviews
Gunnersaurus, Arsenal's official mascot fired, returns
Guinness 0.0 recalled two weeks after launch
Gyms closed
Gambling online up
Goats take over empty Welsh streets
Jimmy Greaves, footballer (d)
Rudy Giuliani, flatulence during Michigan hearing

H
Hospitals
Maggie Hambling's nude statue of Mary Wollstonecraft
Hospitality industry hit
Home schooling
Kamala Harris VP-elect
House price inflation
Herd immunity
Matt Hancock "cries" on TV re. vaccine news
"HMP Manchester" -Manchester Uni students' lockdown sign
Hair dye runs down Rudy Giuliani's face

Hands, face, space

Hong Kong pro-democracy activists on riot charge

Haircuts, lack thereof

Gerard Houllier, football manager (d)

Happy Birthday, instruction to sing twice while washing hands

Dido Harding oversees virus testing scheme failure, gets promoted

Hazmat suits

Hammersmith Bridge closed

Tom Hanks, first celeb to announce he'd caught virus

Toots Hibbert, musician (d)

Lewis Hamilton wins seventh F1 World Championship

Eddie Van Halen, musician (d)

Lewis Hamilton loses battle to stop 128 year old Hamilton watch co. using name

Ian Holm, actor (d)

Ken Hensley, musician, Uriah Heep (d)

Norman Hunter, footballer (d)

Hand gel

Herring, the fish we catch in our waters but don't eat

Roy Hudd, comedian (d)

Buck Henry, actor (d)

Georgia vote recounts (Trump re-lost)

HS2 delayed again

Huawei banned from UK 5G network infrastructure

Shere Hite, sex educator (d)

Hydroxychloroquine , Trump touts as Covid prevention

Matt Hancock's publican neighbour wins £30m contract for test kit vials

HGV drivers stuck in Kent lorry park

Eric Hall, agent (d)

Hunningham Oak, 300 year old tree felled for HS2

Olivia de Havilland, actor (d)

Ida Haendel, musician (d)

Hug blankets, weighted to give comfort in lockdown

I
Isolation under lockdown
Impeachment trial
Iceberg, world's biggest, on collision course with South Georgia
Illuminating (yellow Pantone colour of the year)
Isreal and UAE strike accord
Impeachment, Trump acquitted in partisan vote
Immunisation
Intensive care
Neil Innes, comedian, musician (d)
Intubating patients in ICU
Infection rate
Irish border issue, Brexit
Interest rates stay low
Ingenuity, first interplanetary helicopter, off to Mars
Internal Market Bill, sets standards across UK
The island of Ireland, much repeated phrase
Incubation period
Ikea closes first UK store, Coventry
Isle of White, oil tanker "hijacked" of coast
Independent SAGE, govt. scientific advisors
David Icke, anti govt Covid response rallies
Intu, shopping centre giant collapses into administration
Ischgl, Austrian ski resort, one of first super-spreader events
In-work poverty
Isle of Wight residents guinea pigs for test and trace app

J
Boris Johnson boasts of shaking hands on Covid ward
Boris Johnson catches virus, goes to intensive care unit
Job sharing
Job losses
Job retention Scheme
St John's church, protesters tear-gassed for Trump Bible stunt
Boris Johnson goes "camping" in Scotland, trespasses

Terry Jones, comedian (d)

Jigsaw puzzles popularity soars in lockdown

Robert Jenrick, Housing Minister, approves new homes in Tory shires

Robert Jenrick, Housing Minister, cancels new homes in Tory shires

Stanley Johnson, PM's father, breaks travel ban to fly to 2nd home, Greece

Stanley Johnson, PM's father fails to wear mask in shop

Jo Johnson elevated to House of Lords by brother

Jet ski Romeo, Dale McLaughlan crosses Irish sea in lockdown to see girlfriend

Jet ski Romeo jailed, freed in time for Xmas

Sajid Javid, Chancellor resigns after Johnson insists he fires advisors

Junk food ad ban

Jo Jorgensen, libertarian US presidential candidate takes votes from Trump?

Rocky Johnson, wrestler (d)

Professor Ian Jackson, surgeon (d)

Japan trade deal, first post-Brexit, worth 0.07% to economy: Dept Int Trade

John Lewis closes stores

Just-in-time manufacturing threatened by no deal Brexit

Jupiter and Saturn in Great Conjunction

Stanley Johnson, Boris' father applies for French citizenship after Brexit

Wilfred Lawrie Nicholas Johnson, PM's baby name

K

K-Pop kids punk Trump rally in Tulsa

"The Kung-flu": Trump

Koala in a Christmas tree, Australia

The Kraken: Trump legal team's spurious law suits

Christina Koch, longest female space flight – 328 days on ISS

Knee, taking the

Lee Kerslake, musician, Uriah Heep (d)

Margaret Keenan, first person in UK to receive Pfizer vaccine

Krispy Kreme, policeman switches £9.95 price sticker for 7p carrots, sacked

Kenzo, fashion designer (d)

"Karen", internet meme re. entitled American white women

Kim Jong-un disappears, reappears, disappears

Irrfan Khan, actor (d)

Keep your distance, Covid advice

KuCoin crypto exchange hacked, $150m taken

Kenosha, Wisconsin protests, Jacob Blake shot 7 times in back by police

Kent lorry park

Charlie Kushner, father of son-in-law, pardoned by Trump

Kleptocracy of Johnson's government

Knitting, popularity surges in lockdown

Kicking the can down the road: accusation re. lockdown effectiveness

Key workers

Kernowite, new mineral discovered

Kuno, military dog decorated for valour

Kompromat, theory on Trump's support of Russia

L

Lockdowns

Lockdown hair

Layoffs

Loungewear – at home in sweats

Lincoln Project, anti-Trump group

Locust invasion in East Africa

Lorry parks

Low-traffic neighbourhoods

Light, Trump suggests introducing very powerful light into body to combat virus

Laura Ashley saved from administration

Leeds United lights up Premier League

Lammergeier, bearded vulture spotted in Peak district
Levelling up – Tory pledge to northern voters
Carrie Lam, Hong Kong leader postpones elections
Vera Lynn, singer (d)
Little Richard, musician (d)
Eddie Large, comedian (d)
Trini Lopez, singer (d)
Lab-grown meat on sale for first time
Boris Leskin, actor (d)
Archie Lyndhurst , TV presenter (d)
Lateral flow Covid tests miss over half of cases
Loop-mediated isothermal amplification test for Covid
Little Britain removed from iPlayer and Netflix over blackface
"Lefty lawyers" Priti Patel's rant re. losing immigration cases
Bunny "Striker" Lee, reggae music producer (d)
Leicester sweatshops found to supply BooHoo
Lockerbie bombing, US charges new suspect
Labour Party leadership election
Larry, Downing Street cat attacks pigeon on TV, pigeon wins
Last Night of the Proms: Rule, Britannia! dropped, reinstated
Long Covid
Level playing field, Brexit sticking point
Liverpool FC Premier League champions
Brandon Lewis: Govt will break international law "in a very specific and limited way."
Dr Julian Lewis, Tory whip removed after winning security committee post
Rebecca Long-Bailey sacked as shadow Education Secretary by Kier Starmer
John Lewis, American politician (d)
Martin Lambie-Nairn, designer (d)
Litter – face masks, gloves etc
Laura Ashley collapses into administration
Nigela Lawson pronounces microwave "mee-cro-wah-vey" on TV show
Martin Lovett, musician (d)

Liu Xiaoming, Chinese Ambassador warns UK over interference in Hong Kong

Dr Li Wenliang, Chinese doctor, first to warn world about Covid (d)

M

Masks

Monoliths mystery

Captain Tom Moore walks for NHS

Elon Musk

Minimony (small marriage ceremony)

Megxit – Harry and Meghan leave for USA

"Most secure in American history" Election official on US election

Manchester Uni students threatened with police over lockdown signs

Martial law – Trump enablers tout possibility re. election loss

Osama Bin Laden cut-out in stands at Leeds Utd

Kayleigh McEnany, White House Press Secretary

Angela Merkel

Mail-in votes in US election

Murder hornets

Modern slavery accusations in Leicester garment factories

Diego Maradona, footballer (d)

Stirling Moss, racing driver (d)

Mackerel, what we catch but don't eat: fish row re. Brexit

Mass testing

Mathematical modelling of pandemic

Mars, mission to

MAGA – pro-Trump

MAGATS – anti-Trump insult

Magwa the mine detecting rat awarded medal for bravery

Mustique, Boris Johnson takes £15,000 holiday paid for mysteriously

Moonshot, govt. vaccination operation relies on "tech that doesn't exist": BMJ

M20 lorry park
Mute facility in video conferencing
Mental health consequences of lockdown
Jan Morris, historian (d)
Mutation of virus
Mouthwash, touted as virus prevention
Mortgage holiday
Ghislaine Maxwell arrested, denied bail
Moderna vaccine
Messenger RNA, novel vaccine tech
Elon Musk
Emmanuel Macron v
Mitch McConnell, Trump enabler
Medicines and Healthcare products Regulatory Agency
Morbidities
Me-too movement
Mar-y-lago, Trump base
Marsh family lockdown version of One More Day goes viral
Theresa May speech snubbed by Johnson in Commons
Piers Morgan gives politicians a hard time on GMB
Piers Morgan boycotted by sensitive No.10
Lionel Messi overtakes Pele's record, most goals for single club
Hosni Mubrak, former President of Egypt (d)
Michelle Mullane, radio presenter (d)
Pete Mitchell, radio presenter (d)
Harry Maguire given suspended sentence after brawl in Greece.
MPs recommended pay rise by IPSA
MPs rise in pay cancelled due to outrage
MPs receive £10,000 bonus to work at home
Jane Mummery, Brexit Party MEP realises Brexit will leave UK no say in EU
Microsoft Teams video conferencing
Gina Miller, Brexit campaigner

N
NEOWISE, "comet of the century"

Nightingale hospitals
No Platforming
National Trust decolonising
NHS badge, promised for staff, failed to materialise for 99% of them
Nantes Cathedral fire
Nottingham Christmas market opens and closes on same day
Nepotism, guiding light of present administration
Netflix ignore royalists' demands re. The Crown fiction warning
Non-essential shops, travel
Nightclubs, closed
Novel Coronovirus
New normal
Alexey Navalny, Putin critic poisoned by Novichok in under-pants
No Time to Die, Bond film delayed
National Rifle Association fraud case
Nitrile gloves
Nasal swabs
Ennio Morricone, composer (d)
Johnny Nash, singer-songwriter (d)
Nigel, Monty Don's dog (d)
" Next slide please" Downing St briefings refrain
NATO alphabet de-Nazi'd in Germany
National lockdown
N95 masks
Nice, France: church attack by Islamist kills three
Negative-yield UK govt. bonds sold for first time
New Kim, racing pigeon sells for 1.6m Euro
National Skills and Careers Assessment, re-skilling quiz
New Zealand referendum - cannabis: no, euthanasia: yes
Northern Ireland Assembly sits for first time in 3 years
NATOME, Trump proposes NATO include countries in Middle East

O

Obesity, covid complicating condition

£108m – suspiciously frequent amount on government contracts for PPE

Olympics in Tokyo delayed

One America News Network, more right-wing than Fox News for Trump fans

Overseas Aid Budget cut by Rishi Sunak

"Next slide please" Downing Street briefings

Olympics in Japan postponed

Operation Stack: lorries parked down M20 headed to Dover

Oxford University/AstraZeneca vaccine

One meter plus, Covid distancing rule

One-way system round shops

Des O'Connor, entertainer (d)

Operations cancelled

Overwhelmed, the NHS

Ockenden Report on Shropshire hospitals maternity crisis

Oven ready deal, Tories claim promise meant the withdrawal agreement

Oregon decriminalises all drugs

Octopuses found to punch fish

Opt-out for organ donation becomes law

Out of office messages

Over promised, under delivered: Johnson accusation

Oasis, retailer falls into administration

Oxygen therapy for Covid patients

Ronan O'Rahilly, founder Radio Caroline (d)

Helen Reddy, singer (d)

Oil prices fall to below £0 per barrel

Offerings left at foot of boarded up Churchill statue, Parliament Sq.

Operation Warp Speed, US vaccine plan

P

PPE

Porn collection worth $29,000 destroyed by man's parents in

Michigan
Pandemic
Parler, right-wing social media site
Passporting – financial activity post Brexit
Pangolin – the source of the virus?
The Proud Boys
Pollution improves in lockdown
"Peace, prosperity and friendship with all nations": 50p Brexit coin inscription
Nancy Pelosi tears up Trump State of the Union address
Pfizer vaccine
Sidney Powell – one of Trump's bizarre lawyers
Panic buying
Priti Patel bullying report
Pardons, Trump pardons friends, allies, family, tricksters and killers
David Prowse, Actor, Darth Vader (d)
Procurement, normal government procedures to avoid corruption/waste ignored
John Prine, singer-songwriter (d)
Paris Climate Agreement, Trump withdraws US
Project Lincoln, Republican anti-Trump campaign
Nicholas Parsons, entertainer (d)
Protect the NHS, save lives
Samuel Paty French teacher beheaded over Muhammad cartoon
Paint job for Boris Johnson's officvial plane costs £900,000
Poverty on the rise
"Plague island" description of UK after new virus strain discovered
Parking charges at hospitals suspended for staff then reinstated
Neil Peart, drummer, Rush (d)
Pret a Manger, fortunes widely discussed re. empty cities
Pret a Manger, Michael Gove spotted inside without mask
Personal freedoms removed by govt., citing virus
Dolly Parton donation helped fund the Moderna Covid-19 vaccine

Polymerase chain reaction tests
Person, woman, man, camera, TV: Trump "aces" memory test
Alan Parker, film maker (d)
Charlie Pride, singer (d)
Charlie Daniels, singer (d)
Plandemic conspiracy theory
Geoffrey Palmer, actor (d)
José Padilla, chill out DJ, Café del Mar (d)
Proning helps Covid patients
Plasma therapy, possible Covid treatment
Period poverty, women unable to access sanitary products
Planning algorithms decide to build houses in Tory shires
Planning algorithms changed
Kelly Preston, actor (d)
Professors all over TV
Pet theft rises
Princess Nut Nut, No.10 insiders' name for Carrie Symonds
Palace of Westminster refurb costs spiral
Pasta, panic bought
Priority booking online delivery slots for NHS staff
Krzysztof Penderecki, composer (d)
Popa langur, new primate species, critically endangered.
Pizza Express, Woking – Prince Andrew's alibi
Pope backs same-sex civil unions
Bonnie Pointer, singer (d)
Steve Priest, musician, The Sweet (d)
Political correctness
Annemarie Plas, initiated Clap for Carers in UK
Jonathan Pollard, former US Navy analyst and spy released after 30 years
Dr. James Phillips, physician criticized Trump's fan drive-by
Dr. James Phillips removed from hospital schedule
Pavement rage, distancing concerns
Pick for Britain, Govt. scheme to get locals to replace EU harvesters
Pick for Britain, 112 of 50,000 UK applicants take up work

Vladimir Putin wins constitutional amendment to retain power
Pop-up cycle lanes

Q
Quarantine
QAnon
Queuing for everything
Quotas, fish, Brexit
Quantitative easing
QR codes for test and trace app
Qualifications fiasco with exam results algorithms
The Queen's Gambit, unlikely Netflix hit about chess
Q Magazine published final issue
Qantas announce vaccine will be required before travel
Quibi, short form streaming platform closes
Quarantini, drinking under lockdown
Quid pro quo, Trump impeachment accusation re. Ukraine
Q&A sessions, Downing Street briefings
QR codes for restaurant menus
Quantum computer outperforms fastest supercomputers

R
Respiratory
Marcus Rashford
R rate, average number infected by each person with Covid
JK Rowling and the trans lobby
Mitt Romney: sole Republican who voted to convict in Trump's
impeachment
Red lines in Brexit talks
R number: average number of secondary infections per infected
person
Russia report released after being blocked by Johnson
Russia report shows govt failed to address Kremlin interference
Jim Ratcliffe, Brexiter, UK's richest man leaves for Monaco tax
haven
Jim Ratcliffe, Brexiter, announces new Ineos vehicle to made in

France
Reclaim Party, new movement founded by Laurence Fox
Rule of six, Covid instructions on gatherings
Kyle Rittenhouse killed 2 people with illegal rifle during a BLM demonstration
Kenosha, Wisconsin, Rittenhouse and Blake shootings, protests
Red tape warning from gove who promised less red tape
Russia, Russia, Russia: Trump refrain
Angela Raynor calls Chris Clarkson "scum" in House of Commons
Michel Roux, chef (d)
Diana Rigg, actor (d)
Quid pro quo: subject of Trump impeachment re. Ukraine
Matt Ratana, Metropolitan Police Sergeant died from a gunshot, Croydon
Paulo Rossi, footballer (d)
RINO, Republican in name only, ie. any Republican not a Trump enabler
Recession, worst for 300 years
Beth Rigby, Sky News presenter suspended over lockdown breach
Inzamam Rashid, Sky News presenter suspended over lockdown breach
Rule Britannia!, Proms kerfuffle
Rolling averages of Covid statistics
Rio Tinto blows up 46,000 year old Aboriginal cave system
Rio Tinto must rebuild 46,000 year old Aboriginal cave system
Ripdorf football team loses 37-0 practising social distancing during game
Rainbow symbols celebrate NHS
Remdesivir, Covid treatment
Rees-Mogg Conga line, oaf insists on in-person voting during pandemic
Rigged election: Trump refrain
Little Richard, musician (d)
Kenny Rogers, singer-songwriter (d)
Carl Reiner, actor/director (d)
Rules of origin, Brexit sticking point

Philip Rutnam lodged claim for unfair dismissal against Priti Patel.
Nazanin Zaghari-Ratcliffe faces new charge in Iran over Boris Johnson gaffe
Rose garden, No.10, site of Cummings' press conference re. Barnard Castle
Rose Garden, White House, Melania Trump's redesign panned
Rolling averages of infection numbers

S
Stickers on floors and pavements advising safe distancing and routes
Super-spreader
"Save lives, protect the NHS"
Samuel Paty, French teacher beheaded over Prophet Mohammad cartoons (d)
South Korea perfect test and trace system inexpensively in February
Statues toppled
Rishi Sunak
Shipping containers shortage
Serco profits rise with multiple government contracts
Serco test and trace scheme fails
"Stand back and stand by" Trump to Proud Boys
Roger Stone, Trump operative jailed then pardoned
Substantial meals needed to order alcohol
"Stop the steal" Trump rallies
The slave trade
Gen Qassem Soleimani, head of Iran's Quds Force killed by US airstrike
Support bubbles
"Star chamber", ERG lawyers examine Brexit deal
Spring, record breaking dry and sunny
Stay home, protect the NHS, save lives, government slogan
Streets deserted during lockdown
Scotch egg substantial meal debate

Serco, gets multiple government contracts worth billions despite performance

Steaming theatre productions in lockdown

Stamp Duty holiday

"Sick man of Europe" after mutant strain of virus found in UK

Alok Sharma appears unwell in House of Commons

SpaceX becomes first private company to launch humans into orbit

Millie Small, singer (d)

Sleep problems often reported in lockdown

Keir Starmer wins Labour leadership election

Bob Seely, Isle of Wight MP went to rule breaking BBQ, ate "half a sausage"

Same-ex marriage legal in Northern Ireland

Schools closed

Stay alert, control the virus, save lives, government slogan

"Suckers and losers" what Trump's revealed to have called US war dead

Singing, banned over Covid

Self employed left out of govt. support schemes

Michael Sheen, actor returns OBE

South Korean football team uses sex dolls to fill stands

Sweden, outlier in Covid response

MacKenzie Scott, Jeff Bezos' ex gives away $4.2bn in four months

Swabs, Covid test

Staycations

Supply chains

Social distancing

Qasem Soleimani, Iranian major general, assassinated by US drone attack

Alex Salmond cleared of sexual assault

Simon Stevens, Chief Executive of NHS England

SARS-CoV-2

Speed limits on many streets reduced to 20mph during lockdown

Scientific Advisory Group for Emergencies (SAGE)

The Stonehaven train derailment

Florian Schneider, musician, Kraftwerk (d)
Saucepans, banging during Clap for Carers
Nicola Sturgeon caught not wearing mask at funeral
Sex, govt rules not between those outside bubbles
Sanitisers
Scilly Isles only place left in Tier 1 at end of year
David Starkey: Historian apologises for 'clumsy' slavery comments
Phillip Schofield comes out as gay
Starlink satellites, Elon Musk criticised for light pollution
Space Force, Trump's new branch of armed forces
Systemic racism
Sanitary products sales banned in Wales as non essential
Sputnik V, Russian Covid vaccine
Peter Sutcliffe, serial killer (d)
Nobby Stiles, footballer (d)
Streatham terror attack
Yoshihide Suga elected Prime Minister of Japan
Liz Sugg, FO minister resigns over foreign aid cuts
Reynhard Sinaga, UK's "most prolific rapist" ever jailed
Special Boat Service deals with tanker hijackers off Isle of Wight
Allegra Stratton appointed US-style Downing Street Press Secretary
Sheep called Double Diamond sells for record £368,000
Squirrel attacks in Queens, NY
Space Force reveal uniform is camouflage, of limited use in space
School meals, food poverty during holidays concern
Snack box or badge: NHS staff offered choice for Covid efforts
Superman shirt, what Trump wanted to wear on 1st appearance after hospitalisation
Sunlit uplands, Brexit promise
Stay safe
Roy Strong bequeaths Laskett Gardens to Perennial
Roger Scruton, philosopher (d)
Shielding re. virus
Self-isolating

Gabriel Stirling, Georgia election official defies Trump, gets threats

Grant Shapps, Transport Secretary caught by own quarantine rule in Spain.

Sovereignty: Brexiters' rallying call

"Spaffed up the wall", money spent on child abuse investigations: Boris Johnson

Jonathan Swan, Australian journalist bests Trump

Smacking children ban law passed, Wales

Andrew Sabisky, No 10 advisor resigns over controversial comments

Samosa, Birmingham prisoner smuggles one in between buttocks

T

Tiers

Tier tourism, travelling from high to low tier area

"This claim about election fraud is disputed" Twitter v Trump

Taking the knee

Tiger King – talked about TV show

Transmission rate

Twenty pound note, polymer version introduced

Test and trace app fails

Transport for London financial difficulties

Test and trace cost tops £22bn

Toilet rolls shortage

Willie Thorne, snooker player (d)

"Test, test, test" WHO Director General

Donald Trump's tiny desk behind which he throws tantrum

Take back control, Brexiters' mantra

Donald Trump claims $70,000 tax deduction for hairstyling

Donald Trump gets fans to send over $207m to "battle election result"

Trans rights

Table service in pubs

Tendering, normal for government contracts, abandoned

Thai protesters v government and king

Stella Tennant, model (d)

Thai king rules from Grand Hotel Sonnenbichl in Garmisch-Partenkirchen,

Trump pauses virus briefing to advertise pillows for supporter Mike Lindell

Today, Radio 4 boycotted by Number 10

20th Century Fox renamed 20th Century by new owner Disney

Tesla becomes world's most valuable auto-maker

Toilets in Kent lorry park insufficient

Toilets at beaches still closed when lockdown ended

Tear gas, what Trump used to clear way for Bible stunt

Anders Tegnell, Swedish epidemiologist

Mike Tyson comes out of retirement at the age of 54

Tele-medicine, virtual doctor appointments

Tombstoning, Durdle Door

Tulsa, Trump rally fails due to K-Pop teens' ticket requests prank

Takeaways, surging popularity

Liz Truss' Japan trade deal worth just 0.07% to UK GDP

Transition team, Joe Biden's, denied access to briefings by Trump

Taliban endorse Trump in presidential elections

Twitter CEO Jack Dorsey apologises for censoring Hunter Biden story

Turkish earthquake

Transition period, Brexit

Thatcher statue unveiling in Grantham to cost £100,000

Greta Thunberg: "Chill Donald, chill!" riposte to Trump on Twitter

Tailgating cameras trailed on M1

Turkeys, 25,000 culled after bird flu discovery

U

Underlying conditions

Unicef care packages to UK

Unicef should be "ashamed of itself": Rees-Mogg

Ultimate Grey – Pantone colour of the year

Urban flight to avoid cramped flats in lockdown

"Unprecedented"
US-Iran tensions
Ukrainian International Airlines jet "unintentionally" shot down by Iran
Adolf Hitler Uunona wins local election in Namibia
Unemployment figures
Tomatoes, tins panic bought
Uighurs in China detention camps
Uber won an appeal to operate in London
University lock-ins
Unemployment figures rise
Unilever Launches refill trial in Asda
U-turns by the govt.
"Unintentional" bullying, Boris Johnson excuses Priti Patel
Uncle Ben's Rice changes branding and name to Ben's Rice
Union Jack requested on vaccine vials by Number 10
UFO videos officially released by Pentagon

V
Ventilators
Vaccine
VUI-202012/01: first virus 'variant under investigation' of Dec 2020.
VAR, football video assistant referee
Vitamin D, to fight Covid
Virtual London Marathon
Verbier, UK tourists stage escape under lockdown
Vienna islamist attack
Patrick Valance, Government Chief Scientific Adviser
Virology
Vegan sausage roll on sale in Greggs
Vulnerable people told to shield
Viral load
Vinyl records highest sales figures since early '90s
Virgin Atlantic requests govt. bailout, denied
Visors

Virtual hugs
Virus variants
Virtual meetings
Vectaerovenator inopinatus, new species of dinosaur found, Isle of Wight
Visiting restrictions
Vaccine sceptics
Virus sniffing dogs
Venice canals run clear due to lack of traffic

W
Woolly rhino, 20,000 years old unearthed in Russian permafrost
Work-life balance
Harvey Weinstein convicted of sexual assault
"World beating": Boris Johnson's promises
Wuhan
Joe Wicks YouTube exercise streaming
Wildfires in Australia , California
Washing your groceries
Working from home
Gavin Williamson's "best country" outburst
Andrew Windsor, Pizzagate, TV interview, sweating, etc etc
WHO
Wind power sets clean generation record for Great Britain
Barbara Windsor, actor (d)
Elizabeth Warren, Democrat leadership challenger
Mary Wollstonecraft nude statue
"Wagatha Christie" press dubbed Varddy v Rooney wives clash
Lynn Faulds Wood, TV presenter (d)
Paula White, Trump's spiritual advisor prays for his re-election
White privilege discussion
Kanye West presidential candidate
Warehouse, retailer falls into administration
"Who gives a f**k about Christmas stuff and decoration?": Melania Trump
Weather, extremes world-wide

Pete Way, musician (d)
Bill Withers, singer-songwriter (d)
World Health Organisation
Professor Chris Witty, Chief Medical Officer
Wet markets, supposed source of virus
Weighted blankets
Windrush scandal
Gretchen Whitmer, Governor of Michigan (D), kidnapping plot by Trump fans
Wimbledon, All England Club windfall with pandemic insurance
Weddings banned during lockdown
Wash your hands
Wetherspoon's boss suggested staff get a job at Tesco
Walter Reed Hospital, where Trump was treated for Covid
Woke, injustice issue

X
X Æ A-12 – disallowed name Elon Musk chose for baby, changed to:
X Æ A-XII as it contains no numbers, Roman numerals allowed
X Ash A Twelve: how to pronounce above name
Xinjiang re-education camps for 1-3m Uyghurs and others, China,
Xi Jinping, Chinese premier tightens grip on country
Xenon gas identifies Covid lung damage

Y
YMCA played at Trump rallies
Yeast – panic bought in shops
Baby Yoda, star of The Mandalorian
York, briefly touted as temporary home for House of Lords during refurb.

z
Zoom
Zoombombing (hacking into a video meeting)
"Zombie mink" carcasses rise from burial pits
Zero, number of legal challenges Trump won contesting election

Nadhim Zahawi, appointed vaccines minister
Jacob Zuma, South Africa's former President corruption charges

For contrast, this is the list we made for the previous year. It's virus free! (May contain Brexit)

A
Article 50
Anti-Semitism
Austerity
Prince Andrew's sex accusations and TV interview
Julian Assange removed from embassy, arrested
Claudine Auger (d) 'Bond girl', Thunderball
Jennifer Arcuri, Boris Johnson's 'friend'
Australian fires
Archie, a baby born
Arctic and Antarctic melt
Amazon (the Rainforest) fire
Amazon (the retailer) shows all Premier League Boxing Day matches
Aramco IPO, most valuable publicly traded company
Abortion made legal in Northern Ireland
Abortion made illegal in some Republican run US states
Abbey Road album turns 50
Animal Welfare (Service Animals) Act
Aung San Suu Kyi accused of defending genocide
Lady Nancy Astor, 100 years of women in parliament
Nicola Adams, boxer, retires undefeated
Andy Anderson, drummer The Cure (d)
Austria legalises same sex marriage
Area 51 Raid, "they can't stop all of us"

Steve Allen, 40 years at LBC

Avengers: Endgame, highest grossing film of the year

Carlo Ancelotti appointed Everton manager

Ian Austin MP resigns from Labour Party

Articles of impeachment, Trump

"King Arthur" by Rick Wakeman returns to BBC election coverage

Pawel Adamowicz, Mayor of Gdańsk stabbed (d)

Arsenal sack manager Unai Emery

Mikel Arteta, ex-player appointed Arsenal manager

Benny the beluga whale leaves Thames

Abiy Ahmed, prime minister of Ethiopia, Nobel Peace Prize

René Auberjonois, actor, M*A*S*H, (d)

"Alternative arrangements", Irish border issue

Tony Britten, actor (d)

Dianne Abbott MP wears mismatched shoes

Dianne Abbott caught drinking mojito on the Tube

Dianne Abbott tells Lab MPs who don't want snap election to "go f*** yourselves"

Apollo 11, 50th anniversary of moon landing

Asteroid 2019 OK, surprise near-earth encounter

Amendments to Brexit deal

Dina Asher-Smith, first British woman to win a world sprint title

A&E waiting times worst on record

Sir David Attenborough polar ship launched (not Boaty McBoat-face)

Ant returns to TV

Jacinda Ardern, NZ PM announces gun law change after mass shooting

Asda threaten sack for workers not signing new "punishing" contracts

Alien turns 40
Altamont Speedway Free Festival turns 50
David Austin, rose breeder (d)
Avangard hypersonic missile deployed by Russia

B
"Backstop", Irish border issue
Princess Beatrice engaged
Brexit: soft, hard, no deal
Brexit Party formed
Brexit Party defections
Brexit 50p coin scrapped after extension
Balmoral, Australia destroyed by bush fire
Ginger Baker, drummer (d)
Bury FC expelled from Football League
David Bellamy, environmentalist (d)
Gordon Banks, footballer (d)
"Britain Trump", Boris re-named by American Trump
Danny Baker fired by BBC over Archie tweet
Simone Biles, most decorated gymnast ever
Bohemian Rhapsody wins most Oscars
Shemima Begum stripped of citizenship
Boo, "world's cutest dog" (d)
"Bollocks to Brexit" grassroots movement
John Bercow, steps down as Speaker
John Bercow missing from NY honours list
Michel Barnier, EU chief negotiator
Joe Biden leads Democratic presidential hopefuls
Joe Biden "No Malarkey" bus tour
Hunter Biden, controversy over Ukraine dealings

Barcelona riots

Geoffrey Boycott knighted, "couldn't give a toss" about criticism

Blenheim Palace solid gold toilet stolen

John Bolton fired as National Security Advisor by Trump

Baby Yoda, Disney TV character

Irving Burgie, composer (d)

BBC announces end of free TV licence for over 75s

Abu Bakr al-Baghdadi, leader of ISIL (d)

Bahamas floods, Hurricane Dorian

Luciana Berger joined the Liberal Democrats from Labour

Birds, licence to kill pests scrapped by Natural England

Boeing suspend production of 737 Max planes, fire CEO

Black hole, first image captured

Bananas, Meghan Markle's sex worker messages on fruit

Banana taped to wall by artist David Datuna sells for $120,000

Bronx Colors Boo Sting, revealed: the make-up Trump uses to stay orange

British Airways 100th anniversary

Benn Act passed to stop no-deal Brexit

Andrew Bailey appointed next Governor of Bank of England

Brazilian Brumadinho dam disaster

Banksy's Devolved Parliament painting of chimps sells for £9.9m

"Big girl's blouse" Boris Johnson on Corbyn in Commons

Gerard Batten quits as Ukip leader

Balfour Beatty's MI5 refurb contract terminated after plans leak

Jair Bolsonaro, Brazil President denies Amazon on fire

Leah Bracknell, actor (d)

Gay Byrne, TV presenter (d)

Britain First say 5000 of its members joined Tories

Blackface, old Justin Trudeau picture surfaces

Fiona Bruce takes chair on Question Time
Jo Brand throwing acid joke row
Baltimore "rat infested": Trump
Bubonic plague returns, China

C
Cricket World Cup final drama, England win
Chertsey tornado
Climate change
Channel 4 climate change debate replaced Boris Johnson with ice block
Climate change, mention of it banned by US trade negotiators
Carol Channing, actor (d)
Jeremy Corbyn loses election
Dominic Cummings, political strategist
Conservatives win election
Thomas Cook travel agent collapse
Change UK (they didn't)
Coldplay release album but no tour, citing carbon footprint
Cats, the film, panned by critics
David Cameron releases autobiography, apologises to nation (kidding)
Chernobyl, TV series
Captured, TV series about deep fake
Jacques Chirac, former French president (d)
Alastair Campbell expelled from the Labour Party after voting Lib Dem
Chagos Islands, UK ignores UN order to return control
Crossrail delayed again
China, People's Republic 70th anniversary

Stella Creasy MP attacked over abortion views

Clapping banned at Oxford Uni to reduce anxiety

China/US trade war

Chlorinated chicken, threat of US/UK trade deal

Ken Clarke MP expelled from Conservative Party

"Cotton candy" exoplanets discovered

"Chopper talk" Trump's helicopter-adjacent press conferences

Dany Cotton Commissioner London Fire Brigade forced out after Grenfell

Kellyanne and George Conway, publicly warring Washington couple

Mark Carney, Governor of the Bank of England announces exit

Christian belief found to have halved in Britain in last 35 years

Christianity embraced by Kanye West, Justin Bieber

Christchurch, NZ mosque attacks

Cassettes make a comeback

College admissions scandal in US catches Felicity Huffman, Lori Loughlin

Cotton buds banned to counter plastic pollution

Cutty Sark, 150th anniversary

Olivia Colman wins Oscar and Bafta

Commons suspended after dirty water leak

Caudrilla halts fracking, Lancashire

Coal, UK's first week of coal-free electricity generation

Stephen Cleobury, organist (d)

Michael Cohen, Trump lawyer jailed

D

Deep fake videos

Windsor Davis, actor, It Ain't Half Hot Mum (d)

Magenta Divine, presenter (d)

Doris Day, actor (d)

Terrance Dicks, writer Dr Who (d)

DUP v Theresa May's Brexit deal

Democracy, used in a sentence with the number 17.4m

Disney+ TV streaming channel started

Dilyn, PM's new dog

"Dither and delay", Boris Johnson on Brexit

Johnny Depp, Native American backlash about Dior ad

"Dead in a ditch" what Johnson said he would rather be than delay Brexit

Dogor, intact 18,000 year old puppy uncovered in Siberian permafrost

D Day 75th anniversary

December general election, first since 1923

Driverless cars carry passengers on British roads for first time

Harry Dunn, car collision with US diplomat's wife Anne Sacoolas (d)

Kim Darroch, British Ambassador to US resigns over Trump tantrum

Hurricane Dorian, most intense tropical cyclone hits Bahamas

Drones – licence required

Dresden Green Vault jewellery robbery

Ruth Davidson retires from politics

"Deep state", Trump conspiracy theory

David Dimbleby leaves Question Time

Jonathan Dimbleby leaves Any Questions?

Paul Darrow, actor (d)

E

Extinction Rebellion

Duke of Edinburgh crashes car

Duke of Edinburgh in hospital

"Exonerated", Trump on Mueller probe

ERG, strangely quiet during election campaign

El Salvador celebrates first murder-free day in 2 years

Elephant statues in Marble Arch highlight extinction plight

Jeffrey Epstein, financier, friend to the rich and famous, sex offender (d)

Aron Eisenberg, actor, Deep Space Nine (d)

Tamara Ecclestone's £50m jewellery robbery

E-scooters, illegal transport seen everywhere

EU flag colours in NYE London fireworks upset Brexiters

Elephant dung gin goes on sale, tastes "earthy"

Energy price cap comes into force

Essex lorry deaths

Electric plane unveiled by Rolls-Royce

Everest, queues at summit

F

Mark Francois, MP "I was in the army, I wasn't trained to lose"

Nigel Farage et al turn backs as EU anthem played

Nigel Farage starts Brexit Party

Fake news

Floods

Fracking suspended

Marie Fredriksson, singer, Roxette (d)

"Fifty thousand more nurses" Tory election promise

"Forty new hospitals" Tory election promise

Fifty pence piece commemorating Brexit scrapped due to delay

Kevin Fletcher wins Strictly with Oti Mabuse

Keith Flint, singer, The Prodigy (d)

Peter Fonda, actor, Easy Rider (d)

Pope Francis gets stuck in a lift

French strikes

Franco exhumed to counter far right shrine

Peter Frates, charity promoter of Ice Bucket Challenge (d)

Fox killed by Jolyon Maugham QC in wife's green kimono

Albert Finney, actor (d)

Fortnite World Cup, inaugural, $30m prize pool

Robert Forster, actor (d)

French company wins licence to monitor British fishing boats

FactcheckUK, Tories rebrand official account during ITV leaders' debate

Fausta, world's oldest black rhino (d)

Fat rat stuck in sewer cover, rescued by firefighters, Germany

"For the may not the few", Labour election slogan

Fuller's sells London Pride beer business to Asahi, Japan

G

Game of Thrones finale

Greenland, Trump cancels trip after suggestion to buy it rebuffed

Greenland glaciers melt

Greenhouse gasses

Glasses, some Japanese companies ban female employees wearing them

Gatwick drone attack

Grenfell tower inquiry

Grenfell, Rees-Mogg apologises for slur

"Gammon", used as an insult re. ruddy faced Brexiters

5G rollout begins

"Get Brexit done", Boris Johnson's refrain

Dominic Grieve ejected from Tories, stands as independent, loses

Joao Gilberto, singer (d)

"Girly swat" Johnson on Cameron in private cabinet paper

Gilets jaunes, French protestors

Zac Goldsmith loses seat, Johnson puts him in cabinet anyway

Greggs' vegan sausage roll

Grumpy Cat (d)

Rudy Giuliani, Trump's unravelling lawyer

Rudy Giuliani does business with company called Fraud Guarantee

Gender neutral school uniforms

Chris Grayling, Transport Secretary's no-deal ferries contract

Eddie Gallagher, Navy Seal reinstated by Trump after war crimes

"Go back home" Trump to "The Squad"

Carlos Ghosn, Nissan CEO, fraud charges, flees on bail

Uri Geller says he "telepathically" made Common's pipes burst

Glue, protesters used it to adhere themselves to buildings, roads, etc

Bruno Ganz, actor (d)

Glacier melt

Virginia Roberts Giuffre, Prince Andrew accuser

Alasdair Gray, writer (d)

Saman Gunan, Thai Navy SEAL, cave rescuer (d)

H

Hong Kong protests

Philip Hammond resigns on selection of Johnson as leader

Lindsay Hoyle elected new Speaker of the House of Commons

Mark Hollis, singer, Talk Talk (d)

Nicky Henson, actor (d)

Homelessness increases by 11% in England in 2019

Lewis Hamilton wins 6th F1 World Championship

Fiona Hill, ex Whitehouse Russia expert demolishes Republicans at impeachment hearing

Home Alone 2, Canada Broadcast Company edited out Trump and another 8 minutes for TV

Huawei banned in US

Heathrow 3rd runway battle continues

Rutger Hauer, actor, Blade Runner (d)

Hillsborough trial fails to reach verdict on police match commander

Lady Hale wears spider brooch during Supreme Court proroguing ruling

Humpback whales rebound from risk of extinction

Hospital parking free for some announced

Jeremy Hardy, comedian (d)

Agnes Heller, philosopher (d)

Prince Harry files suit against Sun, Mirror over alleged voicemail intercepts

Harry and Meghan "Christmas feud", spend Xmas abroad

Harry and Meghan complain about unfair scrutiny in TV interview

The high street, continuing death of, worst year in 25 years

Hungary withdraws from "homosexual flotilla" Eurovision Song Contest

Hedge funds eavesdrop on bank of England for advantage

Human-monkey chimera developed in China

Hottest UK December day recorded

Jerry Herman, composer (d)

Rose Hudson-Wilkin, first black bishop consecrated

I

Impeachment inquiry, Trump

Iranian Revolutionary Guard seize British-flagged oil tanker Stena Impero

Irish backstop

Irish passports, record number issued

Independence for Scotland debate continues

India's new citizenship law "not anti-Muslim"

Idlib, Syria and Russia attacks

Israel, three general elections in one year

The internet turns 30

Idai, one of worst tropical cyclones hits Mozambique, Zimbabwe, Malawi

Neil Innes, writer, actor (d)

Ipv4 internet addresses exhausted

"Invisibilty cloak" invented

Ice loss

J

The Joker, film most talked about

Stanley Johnson, Boris father, calls British public illiterate

Jo Johnson quits cabinet over differences with brother Boris

Rachel Johnson calls brother Boris' rhetoric tasteless and reprehensible

Boris Johnson acted like "dishonest estate agent": John Major

Boris Johnson critic: he is a "filthy piece of toerag"

Boris Johnson describes women in burkhas as "letterboxes"

Boris Johnsons likens himself to the Incredible Hulk

Boris Johnson refuses Andrew Neil interview

Boris Johnson hides journalist's phone to avoid NHS question

Boris Johnson hides in fridge to avoid any questions

Boris Johnson accused of touching Charlotte Edwards under table

Boris Johnson wins election

Japanese Emporer Akihito abdicates

Anthony Joshua reclaims heavyweight title from very fat man

Jaguar Land Rover report record £3.6bn loss

Mick Jagger has heart valve surgery

Jetman, Richard Browning breaks own speed record: 85.06mph

Lord Toby Jug, leader of Monster Raving Loony Party (d)

The JAMs (just about managing)

Japan returns to commercial whaling after 30 years

Dr John, musician (d)

Japan to dump radioactive Fukushima water into Pacific

Jesus statue in Mexico is spitting image of Phil Collins

K

Colin Kaepernick, unemployed US footballer's sneakers sell out in minutes

Eliud Kipchoge first man to run a marathon in less than two hours

"Keep America Great", Trump's new slogan

Kazakhstan changes name of capital city to Nur-Sultan

Kyoto Animation studio arson attack

Judith Kerr, writer, illustrator (d)

Anna Karina, actor (d)

Jurgen Klopp, victorious Liverpool FC manager

Khashoggi murder – five sentenced to death in Saudi Arabia

John Kelly, White House Chief of Staff, fired by Trump

K-pop scandals

Jeremy Kyle Show axed

Jeremy Corbyn anti-Semitism allegations

Jeremy Corbyn loses election
Knife crime records broken
Knife crime warnings on chicken takeaway boxes
Laura Kuenssberg, BBC reporter accused of pro-Tory bias
George King-Thompson climbed The Shard, jailed
"Kraut" Leave.EU campaign ad attacks Angela Merkel
R Kelly arrested on abuse charges
Kurds in Syria abandoned by Trump
Usman Khan, London Bridge attacker (d)

L
Led by Donkeys, anti-Brexit campaigning organisation
Liverpool FC win Champions League
Liverpool FC win FIFA Club World Cup
Liverpool FC unbeaten all season
Labradoodle, Australian breeder rues creating "a Frankenstein"
Kenny Lynch, entertainer (d)
Love Actually parody by electioneering Boris Johnson
Sue Lyon, actor (d)
Karl Lagerfeld, fashion designer (d)
George Laurer, co-inventor of Bar Code (d)
Stan Laurel crowned Britain's funniest comedian in TV poll
Michel Legrand, composer (d)
Leaving Neverland, Michael Jackson abuse documentary
Niki Lauda, racing driver (d)
LEZ, Low Emissions Zone begins in London
Ursula von der Lyon, new President of European Commission
Joe Longthorne, singer (d)
Jacques Loussier, pianist (d)
Ursula von der Leyen, new President of European Commission

Christine Lagarde, new President of European Central Bank

Lev and Igor, Ukraine, Rudy Giuliani associates arrested

Carrie Lam, Hong Kong Chief executive v protesters

Andrea Levy, author (d)

M

Erskine May, "bible of parliamentary procedure" available on-line

Gina Miller, Brexit activist

The moon, far side landed on by China

Yusaku Maezawa offers 100m yen prize, breaks record for most retweets

Robert Mugabe, leader of Zimbabwe (d)

Morrisons rename Brussels sprouts Yorkshire sprouts

Microdosing acid as a smart drug

Microdosing ketamine studied as possible treatment for depression

Theresa May steps down as PM

"My arse is on fire", woman dials 999 after eating curry

Meaningful vote

Majority, Conservative

Emily Maitliss Prince Andrew interview

Minke whale washes up at Battersea (d)

Madonna "sings" at Eurovision Song Contest

Ghislaine Maxwell, Jeffrey Epstein's "pimp"

Momentum, Labour movement

Jolyon Maugham, QC beat fox to death

Milkshakes used as a political protest

Naga Munchetty, BBC presenter calls out Trump's racism

Microsoft awarded JEDI US defence contract over Amazon

Elon Musk wins "paedo guy" defamation trial

Elon Musk unveils "crazy bulletproof truck", window breaks

Scott Morrison, Aus. PM holidays while Australia burns

Measles-free status lost in UK due to fewer vaccinations

Lyra McKee, journalist (d)

Microplastics

Stephen Miller, Trump advisor accused of white supremacy leanings

Mainstream media, Trump attacks

John McCririck, racing journalist (d)

Million March pro-EU demonstration, London

Jose Mourinho appointed Spurs manager

Mothercare goes into administration

Motown Records turns 60

Jonathan Miller, Renaissance man (d)

Macedonia changes name to North Macedonia

Peter Mayhew, actor, Chewbacca (d)

Sheila Mercier, actor (d)

Rami Malek wins best Actor Oscar, Bohemian Rhapsody

Magnetic north pole shifts

Sanna Marin, Finland PM, world's youngest, 34

David Moyes returns to manage West Ham

Narendra Modi wins re-election, India

Operation Matterhorn repatriates Thomas Cook customers

MI6 building plans go missing

Model buses, Boris Johnson claims hobby making them out of boxes

Karen Millen, closes all stores

Marie Claire ceases print publication

Minimum wage rise announced

Barrie Masters, singer, Eddie and the Hot Rods (d)

McDonald' s CEO Steve Easterbrook fired after workplace relationship

N

Notre Dame burns

Northern Ireland votes for abortion rights

Northern Ireland votes for gay marriage

Narwhal tusk used to fight terrorist, London Bridge

North Korea, Trump visit first by sitting president

Natural England withdraws general licence to shoot wild birds

"No collusion" Trump refrain

Benjamin Netanyahu, Israel PM indicted on corruption charges

Benjamin Netanyahu wins Likud party leadership race

"NHS not for sale", Tory promise

NHS A&E waiting times worst on record

NHS GPs, nurses, beds shortage

Liam Neeson says he wanted to kill a black man after friend's rape

Netherlands decides to drop nickname Holland in rebrand

Neanderthals found to have bred with early humans

NATO conference, Trump leaves early because leaders made fun of him

Neutral stance on Brexit, Labour party

No-deal Brexit

Nursing bursaries return

"Nick", fantasist in false child abuse allegations

Denise Nickerson, actor (d)

No platforming, free speech row

Navy Seal pardoned by Trump for war crimes, branded evil by comrades

New Horizons, NASA space probe visits Pluto
Now magazine ceases print publication
A nation divided: summation of present state of UK

O
Alexandria Ocasio-Cortez, US Representative
"Oven-ready Brexit", Boris Johnson's refrain
Jamie Oliver's restaurant chain goes into administration
Ric Ocasek, singer, The Cars (d)
Onanism, Boris Johnson drops Corbyn insult from speech
"OK Boomer", derogatory term used by Millennials
Open University turns 50
Operation Yellowhammer, no-deal document published
Oligarchs donate to Conservatives
"Oldenberg Baby", Tim, survived abortion, dies aged 21 (d)
Terry O'Neill, photographer (d)

P
"Perfect call", Trump's estimation of his Ukraine call
Pink boat, centre of climate protest in Oxford Circus
Paris climate agreement, Trump begins process to exit
Pi calculated to record 31.4 trillion digits
Nancy Pelosi
Personal pronouns
"Pinocchios" given to Trump for lying by Washington Post
Stanley Johnson claims "illiterate" Britons could not spell Pinocchio
Proroguing Parliament
Plastics, single use
Melanie Panayiotou, George Michael's sister 3rd anniversary of his death (d)

The People's Vote campaign, Brexit

Pope visits Abu Dhabi, first by a pope to Arabian Peninsular

Piccadilly Theatre ceiling collapse

Luke Perry, actor(d)

Prince Philip car crash

Prince Philip in hospital

"Penis fish" thousands wash up on shore, California and Britain

Post-truth politics

Potholes

Polarisation of electorate

Premature goal celebrations, VAR

Lord Pannick v Boris Johnson on proroguing parliament

Harvey Proctor wins Met payout over false child abuse accusation

Periodic Table turns 150

Harold Prince, theatre producer (d)

Katie Price bankrupt

PPI

Payday loans

I M Pei, architect (d)

Andre Previn, pianist (d)

Pizza Express, Woking, visit claimed by Prince Andrew as abuse alibi

Martin Peters, footballer (d)

Palmerston, Number 10 cat, sick leave with stress

Joaquin Phoenix performance in The Joker

PewDiePie, vlogger namechecked by Christchurch mass killer

PewDiePie surpasses 100m YouTube subscribers

Rosamunde Pilcher, writer (d)

Permafrost thaws 70 years sooner than expected

"Pornstar Martinis", M&S stop selling after watchdog order

"Porn pass" announced, then delayed

Picasso painting damaged at Tate Modern

Q

Quid pro quo, Trump Ukraine call

"Quite bumpy", Queen reviews the year in Xmas message

Qatar withdraws from OPEC

Qatar World Cup controversy

Anna Quayle, actor (d)

Quantum computing system, first for commercial use, IBM

John Quarmby, actor, health inspector, Fawlty Towers (d)

Queensland drought

Queensland approves Chinese water mining

QAnon, far-right conspiracy theory

Q-Tips banned, plastics concern

QuickQuid, payday lender collapses into administration

Question Time audience member: £80,000 salary isn't even in top 50%

R

Tommy Robinson jailed for contempt

Gary Rhodes, TV chef (d)

Racist chanting at football matches

Jacob Rees-Mogg lounges in Commons

"Jacob Leeks-Mogg", lounging image recreated with vegetables

Jacob Rees-Mogg goes missing during election after Grenfell slur

Red wall turns blue on election night

J K Rowling trans tweet fight

Robert Mugabe, ex PM and President of Zimbabwe (d)

Remainer alliance

Revoke Article 50 movement

Ranking Roger, musician (d)

Refugee children denied protection by Boris Johnson

Russian interference

Russian murders on British soil

Russia tests own version of internet

Russia banned from Olympics and World Cup over doping

Russian interference report not released by government

Dominic Raab "hadn't quite understood" importance of Dover-Calais route

Renegotiation, Brexit

Recycling rates fall

Rohingya people stateless and attacked in Myanmar

"Rolling Stones Rock", Mars rock named by NASA

Today Programme, Radio 4, Tories boycott

Jack Renshaw jailed for far-right plot to murder Labour MP Rosie Cooper

S

Dennis Skinner, MP loses seat

Anna Soubry changes party to stand as Change UK candidate, loses

Star Wars, original saga ends with Rise of Skywalker

US Space Force established on Trump's orders

Emiliano Sala, footballer (d)

Solar Minimum, surface of the sun relatively calm

Super Blood Wolf Moon

Adam Schiff, U.S. House intelligence committee, Trump investigation

Spice Girls tour

Fallon Sherrock, first woman to win World Darts Championship

Nicholas Soames MP expelled from Conservative Party

"Snowflake", used as an insult to anyone who takes offence at anything

Sarah Sanders, Trump press secretary departs, replaced by "chopper talk"

Saturn discovered to have more moons than Jupiter

Sweat, Prince Andrew says he doesn't

Iain Duncan Smith, nose picker

Iain Duncan Smith, controversy over knighthood

Super-gonorrhoea, first UK case

Sibling rivalry: Princes William v Harry

"The Squad", Alexandria Ocasio-Cortez, Ilhan Omar, Ayanna Pressley

Single-use plastics

SpaceX failed rocket launch

SpaceX Starlink, fears of obstruction of astronomers' views of universe

Stormzy's Banksy designed stab vest at Glastonbury

Stormzy in: UK racist? 100% misquote storm

Stop Brexit Man, Steve Bray's daily protest outside parliament

"Super Saturday", commons meets on Saturday, first since Falklands

Sonic boom shakes England as RAF intercept unresponsive plane

Caroll Spinney, puppeteer, Sesame Street (d)

"Surrender Bill", Boris Johnson's WW2 name for law stopping no-deal Brexit

SNP record historic landslide in election in Scotland

SNP leader Nicola Sturgeon delight as Lib Dem leader Jo Swinson loses

Sea urchins, purple, plague of on US west coast

Sainsbury's turns 150

Sainsbury's/Asda merger blocked

Clive Swift, actor (d)

Caster Semanya, runner accused of unfair advantage due to hyper-androgenism

Space crime, first, ISS astronaut accused of accessing estranged partner's account

Ron Saunders, football manager (d)

Tommy Smith, footballer (d)

Kim Shattuck, singer (d)

Carrie Symonds, first unwed partner in 10 Downing Street

State of Nature report: 15% of UK wildlife at risk of extinction

"Sardine" movement, grassroots protests, Italy

Roger Stone, Trump advisor jailed

Smacking banned in Scotland

Peter Schreier, tenor (d)

Surrey train stabbing

Mike Stefanik, NASCAR champion (d)

Rod Stewart unveils model railway

Space Oddity, Bowie song turns 50

Freddie Starr, comedian (d)

Peter Sissons, journalist (d)

Bernie Sanders has heart attack

John Singleton, director (d)

T

Time person of the year = Greta Thunberg (Trump has fit)

Greta Thunberg, climate activist crosses Atlantic by boat

Greta Thunberg gets newly discovered beetle named after her

Trump "baby blimp" flies in UK and US

Trump found to have lost $1.17bn between 1985-94. A US record.

Justin Trudeau caught on hot mike ridiculing Trump to Johnson, Macron

Trump declares national emergency at border to get funding for wall

Trump alters Hurricane Dorian map with Sharpie

Trump guilty of misusing charity money, fined $2m

Trump claims people have to flush toilet 10 times

Trump trade wars

Trump's lies since taking office: 15,413 as at Dec 10 2019

Trump: "I have the right do whatever I want", cites Article II of Constitution

Toilet charges scrapped at busiest railway stations

Peter Tork, Monkees (d)

Trees, 440m promised by Irish government in next 20 years

TVs without signal, Freeview cite weather in Christmas nightmare

TV, free licences to be scrapped for over 75's

Tottenham Hotspur new stadium unveiled

Donald Tusk, "special place in Hell" for Brexiters without a plan

Tesco turns 100

Rip Torn, actor (d)

Sarah Thomas, first person to swim Channel four times non-stop

U

Chuka Umunna changes party again

Universal basic income

Uluru, Ayres Rock, permanently closed to climbers

Emanuel Ungaro, fashion designer (d)

Unemployment lowest since 1975

Umbrella protests continue, Hong Kong

Unicorns, Brexiters accused of fantasies

ULEZ, Ultra Low Emissions Zone begins, London

Ukraine election won by comedian

Ukrainian ambassador's car attacked, London

Ultima Thule space rock renamed Arrokoth to avoid Nazi link

Uyghur muslims persecution in China

US government shutdown longest in history

USA win FIFA Women's World Cup

Ultra-long-haul flights begun, London-Sydney

"Uncooperative crusties" Boris Johnson's name for Extinction rebellion

"Unmatched wisdom", Trump's self aggrandisement

UBER loses licence to operate in London

Vernon Unsworth, Thai rescue diver loses "paedo" court case to Elon Musk

Ben Unwin, actor (d)

Upskirting now criminal offence

V

Venice floods

Virgin Trains record highest passenger satisfaction ratings

Virgin Trains removed from operating West Coast franchise after 22 years

Leo Varadkar and Irish border issue

VAR, "it's not football any more"

Vaping deaths

Venezuela presidential crisis

Paul Volcker, economist (d)

Rebekha Vardy v Coleen Rooney

Gloria Vanderbilt, fashion designer (d)

Keith Vaz suspended from Commons after drug and sex allegations

Virtue signalling

Victoria Falls dries up after drought

Treaty of Versailles turns 100

Jan-Michael Vincent, actor (d)

Voter ID law suggested

Victoria and Albert museum agree to display Thatcher's handbag

Veganuary

Violin worth £250,000 left on train, returned

W

Windmills, "Nobody knows more about them than me": Trump

Allee Willis, songwriter "Friends" TV show theme (d)

Whaley Bridge dam breaks

Women Against State Pension Inequality

White Island volcano, NZ eruption

Wetherspoon pubs post loss

Wetherspoon boss Tim Martin gets £44m richer while criticising elite

Wall, Trump's border barrier

"Workington Man" decides election

WOW Air goes bust

Woke – term meaning alert to injustice, used as insult

"World is tiny compared to the universe": Trump

John Witherspoon, actor (d)

Tom Watson quits as Labour Deputy Leader

Whirlpool washing machine recall

Windows 7, end of support

WhatsApp to stop working on millions of phones

"Will of the people"

Brian Walden, journalist (d)

Ann Widdecombe joins Brexit Party

Woking Pizza Express, Prince Andrew recalls visit

Tiger Woods comeback, wins fifth Masters Title

"A Warning" by Anonymous, insider in Trump Whitehouse book

Scott Walker, singer (d)

WTO rules, Brexit

Harvey Weinstein, sex assault allegations

Charlie Whiting, motorsports director (d)

Phoebe Waller-Bridge wins multiple awards for Fleabag

Bob Willis, cricketer (d)

Baroness Warnock, philosopher (d)

"Wagatha Christie", Coleen Rooney turns sleuth v Rebekha Vardy

Reg Watson, creator of Neighbours, Crossroads (d)

Woodstock Music and Art Fair turns 50

Woodstock 50 festival cancelled

The Who return with new album

X

Xi Jinping v Trump

Xi Jinping v Hong Kong

Xi Jinping awarded title "People's Leader" like of that of Mao Tse-tung

Xi Jinping taken off GQ's Worst Dressed list, publisher accused of censorship

XR, Extinction Rebellion

Y

Yellow vest protest in France

Yutu-2 Chinese moon landing robotic rover

Baby Yoda

Operation Yellowhammer, government no-deal document leaked

Andrew Yang, tie-less during Democratic primary debates

Marie Yovanovitch, US Ambassador caught in Trump Ukraine scandal

"You lost, get over it", Brexiters' refrain

Yamaha TT-R125, Boris Johnson's Xmas gift from girlfriend

Z

Zero: what 1 in 5 of FTSE companies paid in corporation tax 2018

Franky Zapata, first person to cross the English Channel on a jet-powered flyboard.

Nazanin Zaghari-Ratcliffe, still in jail in Iran, hunger strike

Vlodymyr Zelensky wins Ukraine elction

Zambia effectively expels US Ambassador after gay rights row

Franco Zeffirelli, director (d)

Volodymyr Zelensky elected President of Ukraine

Zircon hypersonic missile launched by Russia

Mark Zuckerberg, Facebook free speech/disinformation row

Printed in Great Britain
by Amazon

70890585R00037